//
℞ Prescription for HEALING

June H. Olin

Copyright © 2005 by June H. Olin

All rights reserved. Contents and/or cover may not be reproduced in whole or in part in any form without the express written consent of the Publisher.

Published by June H Olin

PMB 120
2020 Fieldstone Parkway, Suite 900
Franklin, TN 37069
Printed in the United States of America

Library of Congress Control Number 2005902322
ISBN 0-9767447-0-8

Scripture quotations are taken from and used by permission, all rights reserved: The Amplified Bible (AMP). The Amplified Bible, Old Testament. Copyright © 1965, 1987 by Zondervan Corporation. The Amplified Bible, New Testament, Copyright 1958, 1987 by the Lockman Foundation. ** The Holy Bible, New International Version (NIV). Copyright © 1973, 1978, 1984 by International Bible Society. Used by permission of Zondervan Publishing House. ** The Message (MSG) Copyright © 2002 by Eugene H. Patterson ** The New King James Version (NKJV). Copyright © 1982 by Thomas Nelson, Inc. ** The Holy Bible, New Living Translation (NLT) Copyright © 1996 Tyndale House Publishers, Inc. Wheaton, Illinois 60189

Author's Note – In certain translations, some publishers have not capitalized pronouns referring to God and Jesus. We apologize for the confusion.

ACKNOWLEDGMENTS

First, I'd like to extend my heartfelt appreciation to my "Mama," who has never stopped encouraging me to write the Rx books. Thanks, Mom!

Thank you, Barbara Smith, for your obedience to our precious Lord and Savior and for helping to further spread God's Word to this broken world.

To my sister-in-law, Dr. Teri Wunderman, a huge thanks for your many words of encouragement, your profound wisdom, and your insightful suggestions. May God bless your beautiful family and your thriving practice.

Jim, thank you for helping put all this together, the countless prayers and, of course, the unwavering support! I love you, my husband!

To Grandmother Mehan, the most beautiful grandmother in the world, thank you for letting me share your personal experience with the rest of the world.

I offer my sincere gratitude to Pete, my best friend. Thank you for being one of my guinea pigs and proving to this world that God's Word is alive, most powerful, and it really works!

INTRODUCTION

Grab yourself a cup of coffee or a hot tea. Now follow me to my back porch and let's get acquainted in my well worn, yet favorite green rocking chairs. I want to share with you my secret for a healthier body. It works, and with no side effects!

Miracle #1

Once upon a time... The sun was just beginning to rise as I sat on my back porch saying a short prayer with such excitement about the quiet time I was planning to spend with the Lord reading His Word. I had been homeschooling our daughter and hadn't had the quantity of time in His Word like before our homeschool endeavor. With much anticipation, I opened my Bible and began reading. I felt a strong urging almost immediately to pray for my Grandmother. I said a very quick prayer regarding her recent move to Florida and asked God to comfort her during this transitional time in her life. Again, I opened my Bible and tried to read. I felt God nudging me, saying "pray for her." I responded, "Lord, I haven't had much time with You in Your Word. I can pray for Grandmother later once everyone wakes up, but I really need to read and study Your Word right now." As I started to read His Word again, I heard, "pray for her now!" Finally, I listened to the Lord, put my Bible down and picked up my prayer journal and began writing my inner-most thoughts to the Lord. I asked the Lord to be with Grandmother and comfort her because I thought she wanted to go back home to Atlanta and was very homesick. I had just spoken to my Aunt the night before and she informed me that Grandmother was doing fine physically, but was still having a difficult time adjusting to her out-of-state move. After I finished writing my prayer, God released me to read and savor His Word.

A couple of hours later my Mom called to let me know that Grandmother was in the emergency room and was in serious condition. Mom said that about two hours earlier, Grandmother had almost died. She stopped breathing twice in the ambulance and was revived after a concerted effort by the EMTs. I thought back to the prompting of the Holy Spirit, urging me to pray for her.

I went up to the hospital emergency room and saw Grandmother, basically in a coma, fighting for her life. I remembered my little book of Scriptures I had in my purse. I pulled it out and began reading God's Word **out loud** *to her. I would read His Word and then ask her if she understood how much He loved her, and she'd shake her head "yes." Her children said she hadn't responded to anyone until that point. The more Scriptures I read* **out loud** *to her, the more "life" began to return to her body.*

Grandmother was moved to ICU from the emergency room. The following day, I went back to the hospital only to find her back in a coma and on a respirator. I was allowed to visit for just a few minutes every few hours. I knew I had to get God's Word read **aloud** *to her constantly. I brought headphones and a CD with songs about the blood* of Jesus. I placed them on her head, turned the powerful music on, prayed over her, kissed her forehead, whispered, "I love you", and left her room.

It was late and we called the doctor to find out exactly what Grandmother's prognosis was. He said that she'd had a massive heart attack and there was severe damage; he didn't expect her to make it. I felt as if someone had hit me in the stomach and I couldn't breathe. I left the hospital after midnight and doubted the Lord. I didn't understand why He had prompted and urged me to pray for her. I even thought I might receive a call the next morning saying my Grandmother had died.

The following morning Mom called from the hospital. She said Grandmother was so much better and that they had taken her off the respirator. They even moved her from ICU to a regular room! Praise God! I could see His miracle unfold right before my eyes.

My husband and I went out of town for a few days in celebration of my birthday. I felt very good about leaving Grandmother because she was doing so well, and all of her children were with her. We came back on a Saturday evening, and Sunday after church we headed back to the hospital with our four children and a couple of their friends in tow. I was shocked to see my Grandmother in such a dire state. She was grey in color and unresponsive to her doctor and family. The countenance of her children was solemn and tearful. There was dead silence as I walked into her room. I felt scared and saddened. Satan immediately yelled these words into my ears, "She's going to die. She's going to die!!" Feeling defeated, I asked my Aunt what had happened.

She said she didn't know, except that Grandmother had progressively gotten worse over the past day or two.

I hadn't brought my little Scripture book with me, but I knew I had to start saying God's Word to her fast! Luckily, I had repeated so many of them to her previously that I started rattling them off from memory. Miraculously, she started responding, smiling and even talking! Her color changed from grey to pink. She even said she was hungry, and I fed her solid food.

My husband and I went back to the hospital one last time before Grandmother left to go back to her childhood home in Atlanta. We sang her favorite hymns, prayed with her, and of course, read her lots of Scriptures.

It has been almost two years since our Grandmother came so close to her death. She is doing well, and she is a happy, healthy, thankful 86-years-young woman. Many of our family members were privileged to see God's perfect plan unfold. He is a God of miracles yesterday, today and forever! I saw Him defeat death right before my very eyes!

Miracle #2

To begin with, my best friend lives in Florida, and I live in Tennessee. Because of schedules and proximity, we don't get to see each other often. Frequently, I talk with her about my books, and at times she gives me words of wisdom. Unfortunately, she is ill with many infirmities. For more than a year, she has had a broken arm that would not mend because of a rare bone disease. Surgeries have provided temporary relief, yet her arm is so fragile, she hasn't been able to drive for over a year now.

*Just recently, she shared with me the intense pain and discomfort she experiences. I handed her my half-written Rx **Healing** book and asked her to please read the Scriptures **out loud** every day. She read the book, probably not as much as the "prescription" called for, but she did read the Scriptures. She called me and expressed that she really loved the book, even in its draft form. She mentioned her upcoming doctor appointment in which her surgeon wanted to discuss possible options for her, because her broken arm was deteriorating.*

*I touched base with her a few days later after her appointment. She said, "You won't believe this, but after my doctor read my x-ray, he said, 'This is weird, but I think your arm is **healing**! What have you been doing?'" She smiled, thinking about the Rx book, and answered, "I've been reading…."*

I am here to tell you God's Word works! It is alive and powerful and is the only foolproof prescription for living …happily ever after.

Don't believe me or my stories of miracles that I have witnessed, but instead, try the prescription for yourself. Read and pray His Scriptures to your sick loved ones and witness first hand the power of The Almighty God. You have nothing to lose but a small bit of your time. Go ahead…try it – exactly as prescribed and remember don't give up.

It's time to dive into this little book. Carry it with you wherever you go and be sure to take all the prescribed Scriptures at least twice a day.

Please e-mail me at Info@Rxbooks.com with your good news. I look forward to hearing from you! God bless you, my friend in Christ.

PRAYER NOTES
for a
NEW BEGINNING

Today, God's Word spoke this to me_____

_____

_____

_____

_____

I will let go of_____

_____

_____

_____

_____

I will begin by_____

_____

_____

_____

¹²For the word of God is living and powerful, and sharper than any two-edged sword, piercing even to the division of soul and spirit, and of joints and marrow, and is a discerner of the thoughts and intents of the heart.

Hebrews 4:12 (NKJV)

This Scripture is the basis for the "Rx" books because when you are sick (emotionally, spiritually, or physically), you need a prescription for something that will improve your health. God's Word is more alive and powerful than any drug, doctor or therapist. It is life, and contains all answers to life's questions.

If you will use it as a mandatory tool for your life, your journey on Earth will prosper in peace, happiness and completeness, regardless of your circumstances.

Please, I beg of you, read and reread these passages. Get ready, my dear, for a perpetual smile upon your face.

PRAYER NOTES
for a
NEW BEGINNING

Today, God's Word spoke this to me _____

_____

_____

_____

_____

I will let go of _____

_____

_____

_____

_____

I will begin by _____

_____

_____

_____

¹⁴Are you sick? Call the church leaders together to pray and anoint you with oil in the name of the Master.
¹⁵Believing-prayer will heal you, and Jesus will put you on your feet. And if you've sinned, you'll be forgiven — healed inside and out.
¹⁶Make this your common practice: Confess your sins to each other and pray for each other so that you can live together whole and healed. The prayer of a person living right with God is something powerful to be reckoned with.

James 5: 14-16 (MSG)

In other words, pray and believe. Ask other believers to pray with you. Let go of anything that keeps you upset or mad.

You, my dear, are equipped with some powerful tools. One of the most potent is prayer. Pick up your "prayer tool" today and get to work!

PRAYER NOTES
for a
NEW BEGINNING

Today, God's Word spoke this to me_____

_____

_____

_____

_____

I will let go of _____

_____

_____

_____

_____

_____

I will begin by_____

_____

_____

_____

²⁸**When Jesus got home, the blind men went in with him. Jesus said to them, "Do you really believe I can do this?" They said, "Why, yes, Master!"** ²⁹**He touched their eyes and said, "Become what you believe."**

Matthew 9:28-29 (MSG)

Jesus healed two blind men by touching their eyes. But the healing took place because of the faith that these two men possessed. Faith meant that they believed that Jesus could heal them before He ever touched their eyes. That's the kind of faith He requires of us, as well. Before the healing takes place, we must believe that it IS going to happen! That's the definition of faith; believing before seeing the results.

PRAYER NOTES
for a
NEW BEGINNING

Today, God's Word spoke this to me_____

_____

_____

_____

_____

I will let go of_____

_____

_____

_____

_____

I will begin by_____

_____

_____

_____

> **¹⁴In prayer there is a connection between what God does and what you do. You can't get forgiveness from God, for instance, without also forgiving others.**
> **¹⁵If you refuse to do your part, you cut yourself off from God's part.**
>
> **Matthew 6: 14-15 (MSG)**

There are two main reasons I must forgive. One, God commands me to forgive others, which opens the door for me then to ask forgiveness from God. Two, by forgiving others, I clear the passage for health and healing to take place in my body. I read an article recently that said there are seminars being offered across the country on forgiveness. Researchers have found that people who harbor unforgiveness have high blood pressure, heart disease, and many other health problems. So, my friend, let's get this body back into shape by getting on God's treadmill of prayer and forgiveness.

PRAYER NOTES
for a
NEW BEGINNING

Today, God's Word spoke this to me _____

_____

_____

_____

_____

I will let go of _____

_____

_____

_____

_____

I will begin by _____

_____

_____

_____

> ²"But for you who fear my name, the Sun of Righteousness will rise with healing in his wings. And you will go free, leaping with joy like calves let out to pasture."
>
> **Malachi 4:2 (NLT)**

Freedom is total release from something that has held you in bondage. Sickness, disease, pain, and not forgiving others can certainly be four walls of a prison cell.

God says if we maintain a reverent fear of Him, He'll release His healing and we'll be freed from captivity. Now please understand, my friend, fearing God is being obedient to Him, and having the utmost respect for Him and His Word.

Grab hold of His promise of freedom. Claim it, stand firm on His Word, and walk away victorious.

PRAYER NOTES
for a
NEW BEGINNING

Today, God's Word spoke this to me _____

_____

_____

_____

_____

I will let go of _____

_____

_____

_____

_____

I will begin by _____

_____

_____

_____

⁴But the fact is, it was our pains he carried —our disfigurements, all the things wrong with us. We thought he brought it on himself, that God was punishing him for his own failures. ⁵But it was our sins that did that to him, that ripped and tore and crushed him —our sins! He took the punishment, and that made us whole. Through his bruises we get healed.

Isaiah 53:4-5 (MSG)

Jesus endured enormous pain and died a humiliating death in order to defeat sickness, disease and sin. Reflect on His sacrifices during your tough times and know that He loved you enough to not only die for you then, but He lives for you now.

PRAYER NOTES
for a
NEW BEGINNING

Today, God's Word spoke this to me _____

_____

_____

_____

_____

I will let go of _____

_____

_____

_____

_____

I will begin by _____

_____

_____

_____

⁴⁰When the sun went down, everyone who had anyone sick with some ailment or other brought them to him. One by one he placed his hands on them and healed them.

Luke 4:40 (MSG)

Jesus heals us by simply touching us with His compassion and unfailing love. Please know that you are worthy of His healing and His love. Ask Him now to place His gentle and caring hands on your broken places, making them whole.

PRAYER NOTES
for a
NEW BEGINNING

Today, God's Word spoke this to me _____
_____
_____
_____
_____

I will let go of _____
_____
_____
_____
_____

I will begin by _____
_____
_____
_____

¹¹ **But the crowds learned about it and followed him. He welcomed them and spoke to them about the kingdom of God, and healed those who needed healing.**

Luke 9:11 (NIV)

Here is another example of Jesus and His great compassion for us. Don't be afraid to ask Him to heal you, no matter how big or small your problem may be. He loves you and cares about every single thing that bothers you. Please bow your head right now and ask Jesus to make whole that which is broken. He is a God of wholeness, and not brokenness. He is a God of health and not disease. He is a God of forgiveness and mercy, and not bitterness and unforgiveness. He IS an awesome God.

PRAYER NOTES
for a
NEW BEGINNING

Today, God's Word spoke this to me _____

_____

_____

_____

_____

_____

I will let go of _____

_____

_____

_____

_____

I will begin by _____

_____

_____

_____

_____

¹⁶**When evening had come, they brought to Him many who were demon-possessed. And He cast out the spirits with a word, and healed all who were sick,** ¹⁷**that it might be fulfilled which was spoken by Isaiah the prophet, saying: "He Himself took our infirmities and bore our sicknesses."**

Matthew 8:16-17 (NKJV)

Remember what I said about His Word being all powerful. The Scripture says, "He cast out demons with a word." The Word here means the Word of God.

PRAYER NOTES
for a
NEW BEGINNING

Today, God's Word spoke this to me _____

_____

_____

_____

_____

I will let go of _____

_____

_____

_____

_____

I will begin by _____

_____

_____

_____

⁵Now a certain man was there who had an infirmity thirty-eight years. ⁸Jesus said to him, "Rise, take up your bed and walk." ⁹And immediately the man was made well, took up his bed, and walked. And that day was the Sabbath.

John 5:5, 8-9 (NKJV)

Sometimes when Jesus heals us, He asks us to take the first step; meaning to step out on faith. Don't keep lying there hoping for a miracle. Get up, get moving and step right on top of your problem!

PRAYER NOTES
for a
NEW BEGINNING

Today, God's Word spoke this to me_____

_____

_____

_____

_____

I will let go of_____

_____

_____

_____

_____

I will begin by_____

_____

_____

_____

⁶**Behold, [in the future restored Jerusalem] I will lay upon it health and healing, and I will cure <u>them</u> and will reveal to <u>them</u> the abundance of peace (prosperity, security, stability) and truth. ⁷And I will cause the captivity of <u>Judah</u> and the captivity of <u>Israel</u> to be reversed and will rebuild <u>them</u> as <u>they</u> were at first.**

Jeremiah 33:6-7 (AMP)

** Portions underlined for explanatory purposes

My dear, if you feel that you are in some kind of bondage, pray the above verse 7 inserting your name for "them" and "they". Also, list your illness in the place of the underlined Judah and Israel. For example, "And I (the Lord) will cause the captivity of (arthritis, cancer, etc.) and the captivity of (hopelessness, depression, unbelief) to be reversed and will rebuild (your name) as (you) were at first." I believe that when we literally pray and speak **out loud** *God's Word with our names inserted into applicable places, we are speaking life and restoration into our bodies and minds.*

PRAYER NOTES
for a
NEW BEGINNING

Today, God's Word spoke this to me _____

_____

_____

_____

_____

I will let go of _____

_____

_____

_____

_____

I will begin by _____

_____

_____

_____

[13]I can do all things through Christ who strengthens me.

Philippians 4:13 (NKJV)

"I can get through this difficult season in my life through Christ who strengthens me."
"I can beat cancer through Christ who strengthens me."
"I can graduate from school through Christ who strengthens me."
"I can love my enemies through Christ who strengthens me."
"I can take care of my dependent loved one through Christ who strengthens me."

Precious one, whatever road you're on today, remember you can make it with the incredible support of Jesus Christ. Please don't take your journey alone. Allow Him to lead you, guide you and bear your burdens.

PRAYER NOTES
for a
NEW BEGINNING

Today, God's Word spoke this to me _____

_____

_____

_____

_____

I will let go of _____

_____

_____

_____

_____

I will begin by _____

_____

_____

_____

⁸As it happened, Publius's father was ill with fever and dysentery. Paul went in and prayed for him, and laying his hands on him, he healed him. ⁹Then all the other sick people on the island came and were cured.

Acts 28:8-9 (NLT)

Many miracles happened during Jesus' life on Earth. He tells us in the Scriptures that even more miracles will happen after He's gone. Yet, we witness very few miracles today. I believe it's because we really don't believe, deep down, that He will heal us! I have been so guilty of this, "praying and not expecting".

He defeated sickness and disease on the cross. Take advantage of what He did for you. This time, ask Him and believe that He will heal you. Rest in the fact that He is taking care of you.

PRAYER NOTES
for a
NEW BEGINNING

Today, God's Word spoke this to me _____

_____

_____

_____

_____

I will let go of _____

_____

_____

_____

_____

I will begin by _____

_____

_____

_____

> **²⁴The people of Israel will no longer say, "We are sick and helpless," for the L͟o͟r͟d will forgive their sins.**
>
> **Isaiah 33:24 (NLT)**

I can't think of a better Scripture in the Bible that more clearly shows the relationship between forgiveness and healing. But the other side of this coin is that YOU must forgive others if you want God to forgive you. So if you want healing and a great relationship with the Lord, then you must forgive others so that you may be forgiven and start reaping the benefits of having a close relationship with our Lord and Savior.

PRAYER NOTES
for a
NEW BEGINNING

Today, God's Word spoke this to me _____

_____

_____

_____

_____

I will let go of _____

_____

_____

_____

_____

I will begin by _____

_____

_____

_____

> **17"Ah, Lord GOD! Behold,
> You have made the heavens and the earth
> by Your great power and outstretched arm.
> There is nothing too hard for You."**
>
> **Jeremiah 32:17 (NKJV)**

Please pray with me for a moment:
Dear precious Lord, you are so incredibly powerful that my little mind can't begin to fathom your omnipotence. I know that my suffering of (your problem) is certainly not too difficult for You. I ask You now as Your child to please stretch out your healing hand and touch my situation. Lord, I ask that Your perfect will be done in my life and that if Your will is for a complete healing then please make me a new person both physically and spiritually. Please restore my health and my hope. Dear Heavenly Father if I am harboring resentment or anger toward someone please reveal this to me now and help me learn how to forgive this person and love them in spite of our past encounters. Lord, I'm not only looking for a physical healing, but an inward restoration as well. I do believe you can heal me. I thank you for your healing and unconditional love. I pray all these things in Jesus' name. Amen.

PRAYER NOTES
for a
NEW BEGINNING

Today, God's Word spoke this to me _____

_____

_____

_____

_____

I will let go of _____

_____

_____

_____

_____

I will begin by _____

_____

_____

_____

[29] He gives power to the weak, And to those who have no might, He increases strength. [30] Even the youth shall faint and be weary, And the young men shall utterly fall, [31] But those who wait on the LORD Shall renew their strength; They shall mount up with wings like eagles, They shall run and not be weary. They shall walk and not faint.

Isaiah 40:29-31 (NKJV)

Please, reread the above Scripture taking in every word slowly and deliberately. Once you've digested these encouraging words of life, then place your name in the place of "those" and "they". Reread the Scriptures now. Read it **out loud** *with your name placed in the text. You, my dear, are speaking strength and life into your flesh! These fresh words of life are much more potent than any administered drug.*

PRAYER NOTES
for a
NEW BEGINNING

Today, God's Word spoke this to me_____

_____

_____

_____

_____

I will let go of_____

_____

_____

_____

_____

I will begin by_____

_____

_____

_____

> ¹**What is faith? It is the confident assurance that what we hope for is going to happen. It is the evidence of things we cannot yet see.**
> ²**God gave his approval to people in days of old because of their faith.**
>
> **Hebrews 11:1-2 (NLT)**

One of my greatest strengths has always been math. Most of my adult years have been spent getting concrete answers to black and white numerical problems. For this reason, "faith" was very intimidating to me. I chose to bury my head in the sand and pretend that "faith" was a part of my Christian walk that I could keep on the sidelines of my life. Satan did a sterling job deceiving me and keeping me powerless! But, and that's a big BUT, Satan did not succeed in the end because I now walk, talk, think and live my life by faith. Faith in the great I AM!

PRAYER NOTES
for a
NEW BEGINNING

Today, God's Word spoke this to me _____

_____

_____

_____

_____

I will let go of _____

_____

_____

_____

_____

I will begin by _____

_____

_____

_____

²⁸ "Lord, if it's you," Peter replied, "tell me to come to you on the water." ²⁹"Come," he said.
³⁰Then Peter got down out of the boat, walked on the water and came toward Jesus. But when he saw the wind, he was afraid and, beginning to sink, cried out, "Lord, save me!"
³¹Immediately Jesus reached out his hand and caught him. "You of little faith," he said, "why did you doubt?"

Matthew 14:28-31 (NIV)

Simply put, do not look at the circumstances around you (in Peter's case – the ferocious wind and crashing waves), because by doing so, your eyes will be taken off of Jesus. Keep your eyes fixed on Him (through prayer, reading His Word, and singing praises) and this will greatly increase your faith (belief in His power). For example, if you have a sick loved one and you are praying for a divine healing, please do not look at the dire situation or even listen to the hopeless diagnosis or prognosis, but instead focus solely on Jesus and what His Word says about your situation. Plain and simple! Believe Him!

PRAYER NOTES
for a
NEW BEGINNING

Today, God's Word spoke this to me _____

_____

_____

_____

_____

I will let go of _____

_____

_____

_____

_____

I will begin by _____

_____

_____

_____

> ²⁶ He said, "If you listen carefully to the voice of the LORD your God and do what is right in his eyes, if you pay attention to his commands and keep all his decrees, I will not bring on you any of the diseases I brought on the Egyptians, for I am the LORD, who heals you."
>
> **Exodus 15:26 (NIV)**

Beloved, the Lord freed the Israelites from the captivity of the Egyptians. In the Old Testament, God would punish people by inflicting sickness, plagues and many times death upon the people. Once Jesus, His Son came, we then received a pardon from God. When we sin (and we all do), we may go straight to the Lord and ask Him for forgiveness; asking in the name of Jesus. Instantly, we are forgiven! Thank the good Lord that you and I are made clean, by the blood Jesus shed for us, every single day!

PRAYER NOTES
for a
NEW BEGINNING

Today, God's Word spoke this to me _____

_____

_____

_____

_____

I will let go of _____

_____

_____

_____

_____

I will begin by _____

_____

_____

_____

¹⁶ **"The name of Jesus has healed this man — and you know how lame he was before. Faith in Jesus' name has caused this healing before your very eyes."**

Acts 3:16 (NLT)

Dear friend, there is so much power in the name of Jesus! Just by saying His name **out loud**, *sickness and disease must bow down to Him! In other words, sickness must come under His authority at the utterance of His name! In everything you ask of God, be sure to ask it in the name of Jesus.*

PRAYER NOTES
for a
NEW BEGINNING

Today, God's Word spoke this to me _____
_____
_____
_____
_____

I will let go of _____
_____
_____
_____
_____

I will begin by _____
_____
_____
_____

> ¹⁷(As it is written, "I have made you a father of many nations") in the presence of Him whom he believed even God, who gives life to the dead and calls those things which do not exist as though they did.
>
> Romans 4:17 (NKJV)

My dear, please read this slowly and ever so carefully to gain a full understanding of what God is conveying. First, Paul, an apostle of Jesus Christ, wrote above that "God gives life to the dead and calls those things that do not exist as though they did." If God does that and we are to be just like Him in our actions, then we should call those things which do not exist (good health, a healthy, happy marriage, a couple with many children) as though they did. In other words, if you are a childless couple and desperately want children, then call **out loud** *the fact that you are a couple with a home ringing in laughter from the voices of your children. Speak them into existence. Another example is, you've been diagnosed with a terminal disease. Speak* **out loud** *that you are a happy, healthy person who has much to accomplish here on Earth. Speak life to yourself, your loved ones, friends and acquaintances, regardless of your circumstances!*

PRAYER NOTES
for a
NEW BEGINNING

Today, God's Word spoke this to me _____

_____

_____

_____

_____

I will let go of _____

_____

_____

_____

I will begin by _____

_____

_____

_____

> **¹²And forgive us our sins, just as we have forgiven those who have sinned against us.**
>
> **Matthew 6:12 (NLT)**

You MUST forgive others for their sins before you can be forgiven. I will reiterate this over and over in this book. God never says that there are some sins you forgive and some that are so distasteful that they should not be forgiven.

I don't know what horrific offense someone has done to you or your family. But I do know that you are commanded to forgive them. This forgiveness does not excuse their behavior. Forgiveness is designed by our Lord to free you from pain and bitterness, which ultimately cleanses you and allows you to move forward. When you forgive, you release that person from the debt they owe you. By releasing that person from this debt, you are able to open up blocked lines of communication to the Lord.

My dear friend, ask The Lord to assist you in extending "forgiveness" to someone. You will not be able to do it without His help. Remember, "with Him all things are possible."

PRAYER NOTES
for a
NEW BEGINNING

Today, God's Word spoke this to me_____

_____

_____

_____

_____

_____

I will let go of_____

_____

_____

_____

_____

I will begin by_____

_____

_____

_____

> **²⁶My health may fail, and my spirit may grow weak, but God remains the strength of my heart; he is mine forever.**
>
> **Psalm 73:26 (NLT)**

My dear friend, your health may fail one day. It may be tomorrow, it could be next year or you may never have major health issues, but isn't it great and awesome to know that your relationship with God will never waiver? It will always be what sustains you no matter what your circumstances may be. Your health can fail, your money can be lost or stolen, and you can lose your family members as well as your own life, but my dear, no one and nothing can rob you of your eternal relationship with Jesus Christ.

PRAYER NOTES
for a
NEW BEGINNING

Today, God's Word spoke this to me _____

_____

_____

_____

_____

I will let go of _____

_____

_____

_____

_____

I will begin by _____

_____

_____

_____

⁸With that, Peter, full of the Holy Spirit, let loose: "Rulers and leaders of the people, ⁹if we have been brought to trial today for helping a sick man, put under investigation regarding this healing, ¹⁰I'll be completely frank with you — we have nothing to hide. By the name of Jesus Christ of Nazareth, the One you killed on a cross, the One God raised from the dead, by means of his name this man stands before you healthy and whole. ¹¹Jesus is 'the stone you masons threw out, which is now the cornerstone.' ¹²Salvation comes no other way; no other name has been or will be given to us by which we can be saved, only this one."

Acts 4:8-12 (MSG)

This Scripture says that the sick man was healed and restored just by the power of the name of Jesus. Say **out loud** *that the Lord has healed you. Say* **out loud** *that He has made you whole and well, and has restored your health and that He has done this by the omnipotent name of His Son, Jesus Christ. Speak these words of truth all day long.*

PRAYER NOTES
for a
NEW BEGINNING

Today, God's Word spoke this to me _____

_____

_____

_____

_____

I will let go of _____

_____

_____

_____

_____

I will begin by _____

_____

_____

_____

> **¹⁰The LORD leads with unfailing love and faithfulness all those who keep his covenant and obey his decrees.
> ¹¹For the honor of your name, O LORD, forgive my many, many sins.**
>
> **Psalm 25: 10-11 (NLT)**

Most of my life, I thought I had all the answers and solutions to whatever problems cropped up. I asked God for help while never really listening to what He had to say. I asked out of habit, but ultimately, I relied on me. If this strikes a nerve, please understand that you are nothing and know nothing without Him. Every day, He breathes His very breath into you that keeps you alive. I challenge you now to start obeying His Word (the Bible) and seeking Him on everything you do.

Simply put, once I relinquished everything to Him and started to obey God, I began to see miracles unfold, not only in my life, but in the lives of my loved ones, too! The key word today is OBEY.

PRAYER NOTES
for a
NEW BEGINNING

Today, God's Word spoke this to me _____

_____

_____

_____

_____

I will let go of _____

_____

_____

_____

_____

I will begin by _____

_____

_____

_____

> **⁴A gentle tongue [with its healing power] is a tree of life, but willful contrariness in it breaks down the spirit.**
>
> **Proverbs 15:4 (AMP)**

Dear one please always speak life affirming words to your friends, family, and even yourself. When your circumstances look bleak, don't claim it and certainly don't speak your negative thoughts **out loud**. *By speaking and praying God's Word over your dilemma, you will witness a marked difference in your challenging situation.*

PRAYER NOTES
for a
NEW BEGINNING

Today, God's Word spoke this to me _____

_____

_____

_____

_____

I will let go of _____

_____

_____

_____

_____

I will begin by _____

_____

_____

_____

> ¹And when He had called His twelve disciples to Him, He gave them power over unclean spirits, to cast them out, and to heal all kinds of sickness and all kinds of disease.
>
> **Matthew 10:1 (NKJV)**

Dear, because of Jesus' victory on the cross, you have authority over illness. You can go boldly to Jesus and ask for healing! You must believe that He is capable of making you well and whole!

PRAYER NOTES
for a
NEW BEGINNING

Today, God's Word spoke this to me _____

_____

_____

_____

_____

I will let go of _____

_____

_____

_____

_____

I will begin by _____

_____

_____

_____

_____

⁶ "No, the kind of fasting I want calls you to free those who are wrongly imprisoned and to stop oppressing those who work for you. Treat them fairly and give them what they earn.
⁷I want you to share your food with the hungry and to welcome poor wanderers into your homes. Give clothes to those who need them, and do not hide from relatives who need your help.
⁸If you do these things, your salvation will come like the dawn. Yes, your healing will come quickly. Your godliness will lead you forward, and the glory of the LORD will protect you from behind."

Isaiah 58:6-8 (NLT)

My friend, The Lord God Almighty is speaking through the prophet Isaiah! Basically, if you follow His ways, take care of the poor and be fair with people, then He'll lead your paths and protect your backside. Yes!!

PRAYER NOTES
for a
NEW BEGINNING

Today, God's Word spoke this to me_____

_____

_____

_____

_____

_____

I will let go of_____

_____

_____

_____

_____

I will begin by_____

_____

_____

_____

_____

> [20] My son, pay attention to what I say;
> listen closely to my words.
> [21] Do not let them out of your sight,
> keep them within your heart;
> [22] for they are life to those who find them
> and health to a man's whole body.
>
> **Proverbs 4:20-22 (NIV)**

Symbolically, these words are written to us from the Lord, our Father. This very Scripture explains why there is a prescription in this book for God's Word. I know, beyond a shadow of a doubt, if you read and absorb His word on a regular basis you will gain an enriched life and possess a peace that surpasses all human understanding. When God's Word is spoken, it's more potent than a massive injection of concentrated vitamins. So my dear friend, wake up and ingest God's Word with your morning coffee. Walk about your day saturating your mind in His ways, and fall asleep nestled in His arms. I guarantee you will note a significant change in your life, both physically and emotionally.

PRAYER NOTES
for a
NEW BEGINNING

Today, God's Word spoke this to me _____

_____

_____

_____

_____

I will let go of _____

_____

_____

_____

_____

I will begin by _____

_____

_____

_____

_____

⁵⁶Wherever He entered, into villages, cities, or the country, they laid the sick in the marketplaces, and begged Him that they might just touch the hem of His garment. And as many that touched Him were made well.

Mark 6:56 (NKJV)

Please bow your head and pray with me:
Dear Lord,

Please give me just the hem of your garment to touch. I want to be healed, restored and made well. You took beatings for me. You died a horrible, humiliating death for me. You have offered me forgiveness for all of my sins. You defeated my illness on the cross. Thank You from the bottom of my heart and soul for all You have done for me. And, thank You for healing and forgiving me. I love You!
In Jesus' Precious and Perfect Name,
Amen

PRAYER NOTES
for a
NEW BEGINNING

Today, God's Word spoke this to me _____

_____

_____

_____

_____

_____

I will let go of _____

_____

_____

_____

_____

_____

I will begin by _____

_____

_____

_____

> ³ If you, O LORD , kept a record of sins, O Lord, who could stand? ⁴But with you there is forgiveness; therefore you are feared.

Psalm 130:3-4 (NIV)

If I had to go to bed every night wondering if I was forgiven of my sins, I would be a spiritual and physical wreck. Thankfully, I don't have to do this, because I am forgiven instantly of my sins when I repent. I am just like that muddy football uniform that my son brings home. When washed in hot water, soap and bleach, it becomes bright, shiny and clean. I have been washed and made clean too, because of the blood that Jesus shed for me.

PRAYER NOTES
for a
NEW BEGINNING

Today, God's Word spoke this to me _____

_____

_____

_____

_____

I will let go of _____

_____

_____

_____

_____

I will begin by _____

_____

_____

_____

¹⁴The strong spirit of a man sustains him in bodily pain or trouble, but a weak and broken spirit who can raise up or bear?
¹⁵The mind of the prudent is ever getting knowledge, and the ear of the wise is ever seeking (inquiring for and craving) knowledge.

Proverbs 18:14-15 (AMP)

Keep on keeping on my friend, don't ever give up! Remember, you have the most intelligent and all knowing Father on your side. Why don't you just strut around for awhile with a cute little smirk on your face and relish in the fact that you ARE the child of the Most High!!

PRAYER NOTES
for a
NEW BEGINNING

Today, God's Word spoke this to me _____

_____

_____

_____

_____

I will let go of _____

_____

_____

_____

_____

I will begin by _____

_____

_____

_____

>²³**And He went about all Galilee, teaching in their synagogues and preaching the good news (Gospel) of the kingdom, and healing every disease and every weakness and infirmity among the people.**
>
>**Matthew 4:23 (AMP)**

This passage says He healed every sickness in Galilee. I believe that when we read and pray God's Word, **out loud***, we infuse ourselves with God's pure breath of life! Inhale His Word, claim His healing touch on your infirmity and savor who you are in Him.*

PRAYER NOTES
for a
NEW BEGINNING

Today, God's Word spoke this to me _____

_____

_____

_____

_____

I will let go of _____

_____

_____

_____

_____

I will begin by _____

_____

_____

_____

> **⁷If you abide in Me, and My words abide in you, you will ask what you desire, and it shall be done for you.**
>
> **John 15:7 (NKJV)**

Basically, if you want Jesus to do mighty things, then you must be living in Him and allowing Him to live in you. Blessings flow from the Lord when your life becomes one with Him. My dear, the way to have this incredibly close relationship with God is to ask Him to come into your life, to confess that you are a sinner and to seek His forgiveness. Tell Him you want Him to be the Number 1 love in your life. Then, to have a daily relationship with Him you must read the Bible every day, ask Him to forgive you of your wrongdoings, and talk to Him constantly, always ending your prayer with "In Jesus Name, Amen." He created you to worship Him. He desires and yearns for a close relationship with you. He is waiting for you.

PRAYER NOTES
for a
NEW BEGINNING

Today, God's Word spoke this to me _____

_____

_____

_____

_____

I will let go of _____

_____

_____

_____

_____

I will begin by _____

_____

_____

_____

¹⁹**The Lord God is my Strength, my personal bravery, and my invincible army; He makes my feet like hinds' feet and will make me to walk [not to stand still in terror, but to walk] and make [spiritual] progress upon my high places [of trouble, suffering, or responsibility]!**

Habakkuk 3:19 (AMP)

Remember, my dear one, your strength comes from the Lord. Whatever your problem or need is today, speak **out loud** *these words of victory, "I will walk, step and stand tall over all my places of suffering because I have the strength of Jesus Christ in me." Say this again and again until it is digested and settled deep in your soul.*

PRAYER NOTES
for a
NEW BEGINNING

Today, God's Word spoke this to me _____

_____

_____

_____

_____

I will let go of _____

_____

_____

_____

_____

I will begin by _____

_____

_____

_____

³⁹"Take away the stone," he said.
"But, Lord," said Martha, the sister of the dead man, "by this time there is a bad odor, for he has been there four days."
⁴⁰Then Jesus said, "Did I not tell you that if you believed, you would see the glory of God?"
⁴¹So they took away the stone. Then Jesus looked up and said, "Father, I thank you that you have heard me."
⁴³When he had said this, Jesus called in a loud voice, "Lazarus, come out!"
⁴⁴The dead man came out, his hands and feet wrapped with strips of linen, and a cloth around his face. Jesus said to them, "Take off the grave clothes and let him go."

John 11:39-41, 43-44 (NIV)

Jesus raised the dead. Jesus gave sight to the blind. Jesus held the hand of the crippled while weak legs were restored. Jesus, at the utterance of His command, required demons to leave people alone! Jesus turned water into wine. Jesus defeated sin. Jesus defeated death. Jesus loved. Jesus still loves. Jesus loves YOU!

PRAYER NOTES
for a
NEW BEGINNING

Today, God's Word spoke this to me _____

_____

_____

_____

_____

I will let go of _____

_____

_____

_____

_____

I will begin by _____

_____

_____

_____

> ¹⁴You are the God who performs miracles; you display your power among the peoples.
>
> **Psalm 77:14 (NIV)**

"Jesus Christ is the same yesterday, today and forever." (Hebrews 13:8) Because He did miracles numerous times, "yesterday" according to who He is, He is still doing miracles "today" and He will be performing miracles tomorrow as well. Take comfort in knowing that He can heal you. Start believing that He will do a miracle for you…today!

PRAYER NOTES
for a
NEW BEGINNING

Today, God's Word spoke this to me _____

_____

_____

_____

_____

I will let go of _____

_____

_____

_____

_____

I will begin by _____

_____

_____

_____

¹²While Jesus was in one of the towns, a man came along who was covered with leprosy. When he saw Jesus, he fell with his face to the ground and begged him, "Lord, if you are willing, you can make me clean."
¹³Jesus reached out his hand and touched the man. "I am willing," he said. "Be clean!" And immediately the leprosy left him.

Luke 5:12-13 (NIV)

Leprosy back then was the equivalent of AIDS today. People were afraid to be around those with leprosy and were repulsed by the sight of the disease. In the medical world, a diagnosis of AIDS is a death sentence. But just as Jesus healed leprosy, there's nothing that you have physically or emotionally that he can't make whole. But first, let's look at how this leper came to Jesus. He humbled himself by falling on his face. Believing, he cried out with all he had, and asked for healing. I think that Jesus saw that the man was completely humbled and recognized his great faith in Him, and Jesus honored his request because of these things.

PRAYER NOTES
for a
NEW BEGINNING

Today, God's Word spoke this to me _____

_____

_____

_____

_____

I will let go of _____

_____

_____

_____

_____

I will begin by _____

_____

_____

_____

_____

¹⁹You saw with your own eyes the great trials, the miraculous signs and wonders, the mighty hand and outstretched arm, with which the LORD your God brought you out. The LORD your God will do the same to all the peoples you now fear. ²⁰Moreover, the LORD your God will send the hornet among them until even the survivors who hide from you have perished. ²¹Do not be terrified by them, for the LORD your God, who is among you is a great and awesome God.

Deuteronomy 7:19-21 (NIV)

Ask God to send the "hornet" in among your enemies (cancer, arthritis, heart disease, lupus, etc.) to drive out every single particle (component) of the disease that cripples you. Ask God believing that He is omnipotent and fully able to defeat all sickness, disease, and injury.

PRAYER NOTES
for a
NEW BEGINNING

Today, God's Word spoke this to me_____

_____

_____

_____

_____

I will let go of_____

_____

_____

_____

I will begin by_____

_____

_____

_____

> ²¹At that point Peter got up the nerve to ask, "Master, how many times do I forgive a brother or sister who hurts me? Seven?" ²²Jesus replied, "Seven! Hardly. Try seventy times seven."
>
> **Matthew 18: 21-22 (MSG)**

I had someone in my life recently that I was having a very difficult time forgiving because the offenses toward me were happening over and over again. I would forgive one day, and the next day this person would slap me again with another painful act. Desperately, I got on my knees and begged the Lord to help me forgive this person for the past offenses and the upcoming future offenses. I cried out and asked Him how do I keep on forgiving and not let the bitterness take hold of my life.

Ironically, this was His answer; take a pad of sticky notes and write down every positive thing that you can think of about this person. And in doing so, your heart will soften, the burden will lift, and the forgiveness will come easier.

I know this sounds crazy, but it worked! Positive words heal your heart, your soul, and your body. Go out today and buy some sticky notes.

PRAYER NOTES
for a
NEW BEGINNING

Today, God's Word spoke this to me _____

_____

_____

_____

_____

I will let go of _____

_____

_____

_____

_____

I will begin by _____

_____

_____

_____

²⁰When the men had come to Him, they said, "John the Baptist has sent us to You, saying, 'Are You the Coming One, or do we look for another?'"
²¹And that very hour He cured many people of their infirmities, afflictions, and evil spirits; and to many who were blind He gave sight.
²²Then Jesus answered and said to them, "Go and tell John the things you have seen and heard: that the blind see, the lame walk, the lepers are cleansed, the deaf hear, the dead are raised, the poor have the gospel preached to them.
²³And blessed is he who is not offended because of Me."

Luke 7:20-23 (NKJV)

Look above in Verse 22. Notice what Jesus did for the people. He loved them so much that He took the time to stop and lay His healing hands on the sick. Plus, He talked to the downtrodden, offering them words of encouragement and He revealed His eternal truths. These miracles that He and His disciples performed are meant for you today. You must believe that He can work supernatural wonders in your life! Without "belief" our prayers are powerless.

PRAYER NOTES
for a
NEW BEGINNING

Today, God's Word spoke this to me_____

_____

_____

_____

_____

I will let go of_____

_____

_____

_____

_____

I will begin by_____

_____

_____

_____

> ¹Count yourself lucky, how happy you must be —you get a fresh start, your slate's wiped clean.
> ²Count yourself lucky — GOD holds nothing against you and you're holding nothing back from him
>
> Psalm 32: 1-2 (MSG)

I can't think of anyone who would not like to have an eraser as one of their life's tools. I'd start by erasing some of those teenage words that came out of my mouth. I'd continue on erasing many "below the belt" words to my husband and some of my less-than-stellar thoughts toward really annoying drivers. Unfortunately, there are no real-life erasers, so we need the mighty hand of forgiveness which is a free gift from our Father, Jesus Christ. All you have to do is ask to be forgiven and turn your back on the offense. You automatically receive a clean slate and a fresh start.

PRAYER NOTES
for a
NEW BEGINNING

Today, God's Word spoke this to me _____

_____

_____

_____

_____

I will let go of _____

_____

_____

_____

_____

I will begin by _____

_____

_____

_____

⁵Then he said, "Imagine what would happen if you went to a friend in the middle of the night and said, 'Friend, lend me three loaves of bread. ⁶An old friend traveling through just showed up, and I don't have a thing on hand.'"
⁷"The friend answers from his bed, 'Don't bother me. The door's locked; my children are all down for the night; I can't get up to give you anything'"
⁸"But let me tell you, even if he won't get up because he's a friend, if you stand your ground, knocking and waking all the neighbors, he'll finally get up and get you whatever you need.
⁹Here's what I'm saying: Ask and you'll get; Seek and you'll find; Knock and the door will open.
¹⁰Don't bargain with God. Be direct. Ask for what you need. This is not a cat-and-mouse, hide-and-seek game we're in."

Luke 11: 5-10 (MSG)

Have you ever had a child grabbing at your arm? "Mommy please, get this. Get that. I want this. I want that." Eventually you give in. That's what you are to do with God. Keep on tuggin', askin' and knockin' until you get His answer. Don't give in to Satan or ever give up on God.

PRAYER NOTES
for a
NEW BEGINNING

Today, God's Word spoke this to me_____

_____

_____

_____

_____

I will let go of_____

_____

_____

_____

_____

I will begin by_____

_____

_____

_____

> [20]So Jesus said to them, "Because of your unbelief; for assuredly, I say to you, if you have faith as a mustard seed, you will say to this mountain, 'Move from here to there,' and it will move; and nothing will be impossible for you."
>
> **Matthew 17:20 (NKJV)**

Say **out loud** *to your infirmity or problem, "move you spirit of disease (cancer, depression, etc) away from me... leave me alone... you have no more power or authority over my body. In the name of Jesus, I command you to go far away from me!" (other verses to look at: 2 Corinthians 4:13, Psalm 116:10)*

My dear, speak these authoritative words two to three times per day, exercising your faith and as God promises above, you'll see mountains crumble, sickness and disease defeated and lives forever changed. Be bold in your God-given power and authority.

PRAYER NOTES
for a
NEW BEGINNING

Today, God's Word spoke this to me _____

_____

_____

_____

_____

I will let go of _____

_____

_____

_____

_____

I will begin by _____

_____

_____

_____

¹⁶You have not chosen Me, but I have chosen you and I have appointed you [I have planted you], that you might go and bear fruit and keep on bearing, and that your fruit may be lasting [that it may remain, abide], so that whatever you ask the Father in My Name [as presenting all that I AM], He may give it to you.

John 15:16 (AMP)

OK dear, sit still for a moment and take this in. The Lord says He will give to you whatever you ask of Him, BUT, you must do something first. He says, you must bear fruit and keep on bearing the fruit of the Spirit, which is love, joy, peace, patience, kindness, goodness, faithfulness, gentleness, and self-control. When someone squeezes your fruit, do some of the above virtues come out or does something not so fresh seep out? By walking in the Spirit, and operating in the fruits of His Spirit, you are not only pleasing God; you are opening up Heaven's floodgates for abundant blessings.

The way to bear good fresh fruit is to ask God to help you walk daily in the Spirit rather than in the flesh!

PRAYER NOTES
for a
NEW BEGINNING

Today, God's Word spoke this to me _____

_____

_____

_____

_____

I will let go of _____

_____

_____

_____

_____

I will begin by _____

_____

_____

_____

⁷ And lest I should be exalted above measure by the abundance of the revelations, a thorn in the flesh was given to me, a messenger of Satan to buffet me, lest I be exalted above measure. ⁸Concerning this thing I pleaded with the Lord three times that it might depart from me. ⁹And He said to me, "My grace is sufficient for you, for My strength is made perfect in weakness." Therefore most gladly I will rather boast in my infirmities, that the power of Christ may rest upon me.

2 Corinthians 12:7-9 (NKJV)

You may have a thorn in your flesh right now. It could be a physical infirmity or an emotional pain that lingers. By all means, ask God to heal you of this aggravation. If you don't receive a healing, then ask Him to demonstrate to you His reasoning so that you can grow and mature through His wisdom. He may tell you or He may just say "trust Me my dear, I have your best interest at heart, always."

PRAYER NOTES
for a
NEW BEGINNING

Today, God's Word spoke this to me _____

_____

_____

_____

_____

I will let go of _____

_____

_____

_____

_____

I will begin by _____

_____

_____

_____

> **²²And whatever you ask for in prayer, having faith and [really] believing, you will receive.**
>
> **Matthew 21:22 (AMP)**

Beloved, this beautifully inspired Scripture does not mean that you will get exactly what you ask for because you petitioned and believed for your answer. Make sure that what you ask for lines up with God's Word: meaning check the Bible to be sure you are asking within God's will. For example, my dear husband was inspired by God to move our family away from a city I had grown to love and cherish. I most vehemently opposed moving away from my "comfortable" neighborhood and church. Now listen, my dear one, I could have prayed and asked God to stop us from moving. Believe me, I wanted to spout that very prayer, but more than making myself happy and comfy, I desired to please God. So I prayed, Lord let Your will be done regarding this move. God had a very specific purpose in moving us and He revealed it to us within a year of our move. His plan was perfect for us and we knew beyond a shadow of a doubt our obedience had paid off. He will not lead you astray even though sometimes it seems that's the very direction you are heading…astray!

Please don't get me wrong, God yearns to meet your needs in addition to your desires. Ask of Him always according to His perfect will in your life. Give Him the keys to your car and just sit back in His care and enjoy the ride!

PRAYER NOTES
for a
NEW BEGINNING

Today, God's Word spoke this to me _____
_____
_____
_____
_____

I will let go of _____
_____
_____
_____
_____

I will begin by _____
_____
_____
_____

> ²³Jesus said to him,
> "If you can believe,
> all things are possible to
> him who believes."
> **Mark 9:23 (NKJV)**

My precious friend, please don't ever give up!

If you are looking only to earthly remedies for your physical and emotional illnesses, you are missing THE most important ingredient to your healing process. Jesus Christ. This is not to say that you should not consult and rely on medical experts for help with your illnesses. But no matter what you are told, remember that your Father is the Chief Physician, and the Ultimate Healer.

Nothing is impossible with God, so don't ever give up!

PRAYER NOTES
for a
NEW BEGINNING

Today, God's Word spoke this to me _____

_____

_____

_____

_____

I will let go of _____

_____

_____

_____

_____

I will begin by _____

_____

_____

_____

³⁷Judge not [neither pronouncing judgment nor subjecting to censure], and you will not be judged; do not condemn and pronounce guilty, and you will not be condemned and pronounced guilty; acquit and forgive and release (give up resentment, let it drop), and you will be acquitted and forgiven and released.

Luke 6:37 (AMP)

Drop it, my dear. Drop it. Whatever you are holding onto, drop it. Don't think about it, talk about it or dwell on it. When it comes up in your head, or out of your mouth, stop it dead in its tracks, the thoughts of bitterness, anger, resentment and unforgiveness. Our bodies were not made to deal with these things. That's why our bodies get sick when we hang onto the past. So for the sake of your physical health, release all that "junk" to God.

PRAYER NOTES
for a
NEW BEGINNING

Today, God's Word spoke this to me_____

_____

_____

_____

_____

I will let go of_____

_____

_____

_____

_____

I will begin by_____

_____

_____

_____

> **¹⁴And my people, my God-defined people, respond by humbling themselves, praying, seeking my presence, and turning their backs on their wicked lives, I'll be there ready for you: I'll listen from heaven, forgive their sins, and restore their land to health.**
>
> 2 Chronicles 7:14 (MSG)

My friend, you must do what is right in order to get what is right. The emphasis is on "you must do". I remember a time in my life that I asked, begged and pleaded for help with an issue with which I was so desperately wrestling. Year after year, it seemed I never got relief or help with this problem. Finally, through Scripture, and the conviction of the Holy Spirit, my eyes were opened to the truth. The truth was I needed to start doing rather than asking. The doing that God required of me was to humble myself, break down the haughty attitudes, and turn my back on my old disgusting ways so that God could hear my voice and answer my prayer.

PRAYER NOTES
for a
NEW BEGINNING

Today, God's Word spoke this to me _____

_____

_____

_____

_____

I will let go of _____

_____

_____

_____

_____

I will begin by _____

_____

_____

_____

> ²**Praise the LORD, I tell myself and never forget the good things he does for me.**
> ³**He forgives all my sin and heals all my diseases.**
> ⁴**He ransoms me from death and surrounds me with love and tender mercies.**
>
> **Psalm 103:2-4 (NLT)**

The only thing you have to do to receive forgiveness of your sins is ask God with a genuine heart to forgive you and He instantly forgives you. You can't do anything bad enough not to receive His forgiveness. Believe me, my friend, I have out-sinned you all! If He forgives me, then you're a "shoo-in". Seriously, He removes your sin, as far as the "east is from the west."

Please take a moment right now, and ask for His forgiveness for everything that you've done wrong. Forgiveness…it's yours just for the asking!

PRAYER NOTES
for a
NEW BEGINNING

Today, God's Word spoke this to me _____

_____

_____

_____

_____

I will let go of _____

_____

_____

_____

_____

I will begin by _____

_____

_____

_____

> [14] **"Is anything too hard for the LORD? At the appointed time I will return to you, according to the time of life, and Sarah shall have a son."**
>
> **Genesis 18:14 (NKJV)**

Sarah, Abraham's wife, was well into her nineties when God told Abraham that Sarah would have her first child. Sarah laughed when she heard this! Think about something in your life that seems utterly impossible to change. It could be a physical healing, an emotional restoration, a wayward child, a broken relationship, etc. Do you give a sarcastic laugh like Sarah did when you think about God's ultimate healing of the problem? Reread the first sentence of this verse. Read it **out loud** *while exchanging your problem for the word "anything." For example, it could read, "Is cancer too hard for the Lord?" "No" is the definitive answer! No, no, no, nothing, my friend, is too complicated for Him to restore and make whole.*

PRAYER NOTES
for a
NEW BEGINNING

Today, God's Word spoke this to me _____

_____

_____

_____

_____

I will let go of _____

_____

_____

_____

_____

I will begin by _____

_____

_____

_____

²⁰A woman who had had a hemorrhage for twelve years came up behind him. She touched the fringe of his robe, ²¹for she thought, "If I can just touch his robe, I will be healed." ²²Jesus turned around and said to her, "Daughter, be encouraged! Your faith has made you well." And the woman was healed at that moment.

Matthew 9:20-22 (NLT)

Healing by Jesus Christ, my dear, is for you today. It says in His Word, "by His stripes you are healed." He took on tremendous pain in His scourging and beatings for you and me. Ask Him to heal you and then thank Him. Continue thanking Him for your healing

PRAYER NOTES
for a
NEW BEGINNING

Today, God's Word spoke this to me_____

_____

_____

_____

_____

I will let go of_____

_____

_____

_____

_____

I will begin by_____

_____

_____

_____

> **²⁵And the rain descended, the floods came, and the winds blew and beat on that house; and it did not fall, for it was founded on the rock.**
>
> **Matthew 7:25 (NKJV)**

My cherished friend, please understand one thing. If everything else you've read confuses you, take this one truth and keep it close to your heart. Jesus loves and adores you. His love for you is not based on how you act or what you do. He loves you because you are His most treasured child! Once you ask Him to come into your life, He becomes your Father. You become an heir to the Most High King of kings. So, when Jesus says in the above Scripture, mighty storms will come wreaking massive destruction, BUT you, my dear, WILL NOT fall because your foundation is poured by God Almighty!

I must confess, this is my favorite Scripture! I've had my share of rain, floods and strong winds beating on my house, but, praise God, I did NOT fall (I stumbled often though) because my foundation was solid!

PRAYER NOTES
for a
NEW BEGINNING

Today, God's Word spoke this to me _____

_____

_____

_____

_____

I will let go of _____

_____

_____

_____

_____

I will begin by _____

_____

_____

_____

_____

> ²⁴**Pleasant words are as a honeycomb, sweet to the mind and healing to the body.**
>
> **Proverbs 16:24(AMP)**

I've learned that what I think and speak determines how I feel and act toward others. Did you know that you can merely think negative thoughts about someone and they will sense it and will oftentimes pull away? Start today by filling your mind with positive thoughts, good moral books, clean movies, and uplifting music. Speak encouraging words to your loved ones and even strangers. Take it from me, who has to learn most everything the hard way, your new attitude will make a significant difference in your mental and physical well being.

Rx

Titles by
June H. Olin

Rx for Happiness
Rx for Healing
Rx for Raising Teens

Watch for these upcoming titles:

Rx for Overcoming Fear
Rx for Financial Prosperity
Rx for Weight Control

For more information on ordering these books, write to:

Rx Books
PMB120
2020 Fieldstone Pkwy, Suite 900
Franklin, Tennessee 37069

Or e-mail Info@Rxbooks.com
www.Rxbooks.com